A Christmas Treasury

Illustrated by Eric Kincaid and Gavin Rowe

BRIMAX

ISBN 1 85854 787 3
Published by Brimax Books Ltd, Newmarket,
England, CB8 7AU 1998.
Printed in Spain.

Contents

Jack Frost   *Cecily Pike*   8

The Snow Queen   *Hans Christian Andersen*   9

The Robin   *Thomas Hardy*   23

The Night Before Christmas   *Clement C. Moore*   24

The Wind in the Willows   *Kenneth Grahame*   32

The Three Kings   *Henry Wadsworth Longfellow*   46

The Little Match Girl   *Hans Christian Andersen*   50

The North Wind Doth Blow   *Anonymous*   54

A Christmas Carol   *Charles Dickens*   56

Jack Frost

Look out! look out!
Jack Frost is about!
He's after our fingers and toes;
And, all through the night,
The gay little sprite
Is working where nobody knows.

He'll climb each tree,
So nimble is he,
His silvery powder he'll shake;
To windows he'll creep,
And while we're asleep,
Such wonderful pictures he'll make.

Across the grass
He'll merrily pass,
And change all its greenness to white;
Then home he will go,
And laugh, 'Ho! ho! ho!
What fun I have had in the night!'

Cecily Pike

8

The Snow Queen

This is a story about a little boy called Kay and his friend, Gerda. But the tale really begins with a magician with a magic mirror. This mirror would shrink everything that was good and beautiful into almost nothing, while ugly and unpleasant things were increased in size, so that they looked even worse than they did before. Now one day his assistants took the mirror and flew with it into the sky. Somehow they let it slip from their hands, and it fell down to earth and shattered into a thousand pieces. Several of these little pieces of mirror flew straight into people's eyes, making everything they looked at seem twisted. But the worst thing of all was when a little splinter of the mirror flew into someone's heart. Immediately, the heart would become as cold and hard as ice.

This is what happened to the little boy, Kay, as you shall hear. Kay and Gerda lived next door to one another. In the summer they would play together, or sit on their two little stools in the bright sunshine, laughing and chatting among the roses that grew everywhere. In the winter, when it was too cold to go outside, they would sit at the window and smile at each other through the frosted glass where they had melted a little hole.

One evening, when Kay was looking out of the window, he saw a huge snowflake drift down to a snow-filled flowerpot. The flake grew larger and larger until at last it took on the shape of a beautiful lady dressed in white. Her ice-cold eyes gleamed like stars, and her gown glittered with frost. She was very beautiful. She beckoned to Kay, but he backed away, frightened.

By the time spring came round again, Kay had forgotten all about the Snow Queen. He played with Gerda in the springtime and in the warm summer days that followed. They could not have been happier. Then, one day, as they were both sitting under the shade of a tree, Kay suddenly cried out.

"There's something in my eye! And oh, I have such a pain round my heart."

He did not know it, but two splinters from the Magic Mirror had flown into his eye and pierced his heart.

"Oh, what's the matter?" cried Gerda. "You look so pale and strange. Are you hurt?"

Kay looked at his friend with ice-cold eyes. "Oh don't fuss," he snapped. "I'm all right. It's just you that looks terribly ugly."

Poor Gerda! Kay had never spoken to her like this before. And as the summer wore on, the Magic Mirror's evil power took hold of him, Kay became a different boy. Gone was the kind and caring friend Gerda had known. Kay laughed at people and mimicked them, not caring if he upset them or not. And most of all, he laughed at Gerda.

When winter arrived, Kay longed to go out into the snow. He

dressed up warmly, took his sledge, and called out to Gerda, "I'm off to the village square. The other boys are going sledging."

"Can I come too?"

"No, of course you can't. You're only a silly, little girl."

When Kay arrived in the square, he found the other boys tying their sledges to the farmer's carts and gliding along in the snow behind them.

'What fun!' thought Kay. When a tall, white-cloaked figure drew up in a big, white sledge, Kay tied his little sledge to the big one. Off they went through the snowy streets of the town!

Very soon, they had passed through the city gates, and sped onwards towards the forest. The snow began to fall very thickly, and the star shaped snowflakes grew bigger and bigger. At first Kay was excited, but very soon he wanted to go home. With frozen fingers, he tried to unhitch his little sledge from the big one, but he could not manage it. Very frightened, he cried out.

The big sledge stopped, and the white-clad figure turned around to look at him. It was the Snow Queen, the beautiful lady he had seen the winter before!

"Poor little boy," she said to him. "Come up beside me and I'll wrap you in my fur-rug to keep you warm."

Kay climbed up, and the Snow Queen put her arm around him. He began to feel sleepy.

'I must go back to Grandmother,' he thought. But the Snow Queen gave him an ice-cold kiss; and the little boy's heart, already cold with the splinter from the Magic Mirror, felt icier still. But soon he began to get used to the cold. He felt better, and all thoughts of home, Grandmother, and his friend, Gerda faded. He saw only the beautiful Snow Queen, with her white, fur-lined cloak, and the glittering snowflakes clinging to her dress.

And so they glided onwards through the dark night, through the forests where wolves howled, and across snow-spangled plains.

Very soon, Kay drifted off to sleep, with the Snow Queen's arms around him.

Back at home, Gerda was trying to find out what had happened to Kay. The boys told her he had driven off at the back of a big, white sledge, but no one knew the rider. And though she and Kay's grandmother searched for him all through the winter, they did not find him.

Everyone now thought that Kay was dead, but Gerda did not believe it. When spring came around once again, she set off to look for him.

First she went to the river. Had it carried Kay off downstream? She stepped into a little boat, which gently floated away, carrying Gerda with it. She drifted downstream, past green fields where sheep grazed, until at last she caught sight of a little cottage with a garden full of roses. Gerda's eyes filled with tears, for she could not help remembering the roses that grew back at home in the garden where she and Kay used to play on summer evenings.

'Perhaps someone is at home,' thought Gerda. 'I am so hungry.' She called out, and immediately the cottage door opened. An old lady, bent with age, and carrying a stick came out. She was wearing a beautiful, large hat with flowers on it. She reached out over the river with her stick and pulled Gerda to the bank.

"What are you doing here, little girl?" the old lady asked, and Gerda told her all about her quest to find Kay. "Has he passed this way?" she asked, and the old lady shook her head.

"Not yet," she said, "but why not come in and rest before you continue your journey? You can see how pretty it is here, and my little cottage is very comfortable."

13

"It's lovely," said Gerda. "It reminds me so much of the garden at home - and of Kay."

The old lady took Gerda by the hand and they went inside. It was a beautiful cottage. The sunlight streamed through the windows onto a big bowl of cherries on the table.

"Help yourself," said the old lady. Gerda sat down, and the old lady combed the little girl's hair.

"I have always longed for a child like this," the old lady sighed to herself. "I would like her to live with me." The old lady was a witch, and as she combed Gerda's hair, she wove a spell to make her forget all about her journey to find Kay. However, she knew that if Gerda saw the roses in the garden again, she would remember everything.

The witch went out into the garden and waved her stick over the rose bushes. They immediately sank down under the soil, and no one could tell that they had ever grown there. In their place, the witch put every other type of beautiful flower.

For a while, Gerda played happily in the garden. When she was tired, the old lady tucked her into a little bed, with silk sheets. Gerda slept soundly till morning, with not a thought of Kay in her mind at all.

The next day she was again out in the garden. Every now and again, she stopped and frowned. There was something not quite right - something was missing…

Then Gerda caught sight of the old lady's hat. It had roses on it.

"I know," she cried. "There were roses - but where have they gone?" Gerda was very sad that the roses had disappeared, and she began to cry. Her tears fell on a spot where a rose bush had grown. The little bush sprang up and flowered in front of her eyes.

Immediately she remembered everything. She could not stay with the old woman a minute longer. She must continue looking for Kay.

"Have you seen him?" she asked the rose-bush, but it told her that deep down in the earth there was no sign of her little friend.

"He is not dead then," she said, and she ran around the garden, asking each flower if they knew anything about what had happened to Kay. But though each flower told her a magical story, not one could tell her where Kay could be found.

'I must go now,' thought Gerda. 'Before the old lady can keep me a minute longer.' And she ran quickly out of the garden and away from the cottage. She walked on for a long time. She noticed that the weather was turning colder and colder, and that snow was beginning to fall. Suddenly she caught sight of a Raven sitting on the bare branch of a tree.

"Have you seen my friend, Kay?" she asked. "Has a little boy passed this way?"

"It is possible that I have seen him," replied the Raven. "But I have bad news for you. I think he has left you for a Princess."

"A Princess!"

"This Princess," said the Raven, "is well-known for her cleverness and wit. Since she needed someone who was equally clever to talk with her, young men from all over the kingdom came to the Palace. Though they seemed lively and handsome enough, not one of them was as clever as the Princess - until one day a boy arrived at the Palace. He had long, blond hair, but wore the clothes of a peasant."

"That sounds just like Kay!" cried Gerda, in excitement.

"Anyway," went on the Raven, "this boy came to the Princess. He was so handsome, clever and lively that the Princess fell for him at once. And he liked her, too. Believe me, this is all true, for I have a Raven friend within the Palace who has told me all about it."

"Oh, this is certainly Kay!" cried Gerda. "You must let me into the Palace to see him. Once he knows I am here, he will come immediately."

"I will certainly take you there," said the Raven. "And my friend from the Palace will lead you to your friend by a back staircase, for no one will let you in at the main entrance, because you look so shabby."

Gerda followed behind the Raven who flapped and fluttered his way to the Palace and through the grounds. His Raven friend had left a back door open for them, and in they went.

'Oh, how I long to see him at last!' thought Gerda. 'How pleased he will be that I've come so far to find him. How he will long to be home with me once again, and see the rose-trees, and his dear grandmother!'

They went along a corridor and up a grand staircase. Gerda gasped with wonder at all the grand rooms they passed through. At last they came to the Princess's own room, and Gerda saw a young man standing at the window with the Princess.

"Kay!" she cried, and ran forward. The young man turned, but it was not Kay at all! Gerda burst into tears because she was so unhappy. She told the Princess all that had happened to her, and how the Raven had helped her to find Kay.

"But we were wrong," she sobbed. "He isn't here at all."

The Princess smiled kindly at her.

"Stay here in the Palace for the night and rest," she said. "In the morning we will give you a carriage and fresh clothes. You will feel so much better then."

Gerda slept soundly that night, and her dreams were pleasant ones. In the morning, she found a dress of silk, a cloak of velvet laid out for her, and a little, white fur muff to keep her hands warm. The Princess accompanied her to the Palace entrance and a golden coach drew up for her.

"Good luck," said the Princess, as the coach drove off.

"Thank you for everything," said Gerda. "And thank you, too, dear Raven, for all your kindness."

"I will fly behind the coach for the first part of your journey," he said, and he fluttered along beside the coach for many miles.

The coach drove through a dark forest, but alas, it was seen by a band of robbers who saw it gleaming through the trees. They pushed the coachmen to the ground and seized hold of Gerda.

"Shall I kill her?" said one of the robbers. But her little daughter, who had come with her on the raid, clutched hold of her arm.

"No, Mother," she said. "I want a playmate. Let this little girl stay with me to be my friend."

And because the little robber girl was so spoilt, her mother spared

Gerda's life and let the two girls travel back to the robber camp in the golden coach. As they went along, Gerda told the robber girl all about her search for Kay and the adventures she had along the way.

"Well, now the adventures are over," said the robber girl. "I want you to stay with me and be my friend. I will show you my pets. You'll see what a wonderful time we'll have together."

But when Gerda arrived at the robber camp, she found that the robber girl's pets were a poor old reindeer who was chained to the wall all day, and a hundred pigeons, which she kept imprisoned in one room. The robber girl teased them terribly and waved a dagger at the reindeer's throat.

"I have my dagger with me always," she boasted. "I even sleep with it!" And she pulled Gerda down on a straw mattress and put one arm around her neck. The other held the dagger. There was no way Gerda could escape.

It was a terrible night and Gerda slept very badly. But as she lay awake during the long hours, she heard a pigeon cooing at her.

"We have seen your Kay," it said. "He passed through our forest with the Snow Queen."

"The Snow Queen!" cried Gerda. "Where will I find her? Where does she live?"

"Why not ask the Reindeer over there? He'll know."

The Reindeer told Gerda that the Snow Queen was probably in Lapland, where she stayed for the summer. In winter she travelled off

18

to an island near the North Pole.

Gerda cried out, when she heard how far away Kay had been taken, and the robber girl woke up.

"Keep quiet, or I'll stab you with my dagger," she threatened.

In the morning, though, the robber girl was in a better mood. She had grown fond of Gerda and did not like to see her so sad.

"I will help you find Kay," she said. "My reindeer will take you to Lapland, to the castle of the Snow Queen."

The Reindeer's eyes shone at the thought of his own freedom, and Gerda could scarcely believe that the robber girl was letting her go.

"You will need warm clothes," said the robber girl. "Take my mother's gloves. They are far too big for you, but they will cover your arms."

After giving Gerda food and drink for the journey, the robber girl waved goodbye. Gerda saw her standing by the door, with two huge guard dogs at her side, and her dagger gleaming in the sunlight.

The Reindeer and Gerda sped away over the countryside, through forests and plains, until at last Gerda saw some wonderful, bright lights in the sky.

"Those are the Northern Lights," explained the Reindeer. "We have nearly reached Lapland."

On they journeyed until at last they stopped for shelter at a little hut where an old Lapp woman gave them food.

When Gerda had told her story, the old woman sighed.

"You poor thing!" she exclaimed. "You still have over a hundred miles to travel to the land of the Snow Queen. But I can help you a little - I will write a note to a wise woman I know there who should be able to help you further."

Gerda took the note, and they set off once again. The beautiful Northern Lights shone all around them as they came nearer and nearer to the end of their journey. And so they arrived at the Wise Woman's house.

The Wise Woman read the note three times and then said, "Young Kay is indeed with the Snow Queen. But he has no wish to escape. He likes living there, but that is because he has a splinter of ice in his heart. He is not the Kay you know. The Snow Queen has complete power over him until the splinter of ice is removed from his heart."

"Can't you help little Gerda to rescue her friend?" asked the Reindeer. But the Wise Woman shook her head.

"Gerda has all the power she needs already. Do you not see how she has been helped on her journey? That is because she has a kind and innocent heart. That alone should give her enough power to free her friend."

"Where do we go now?" asked the Reindeer.

"You must take Gerda to the Snow Queen's garden and leave her there. Then return immediately to me."

The garden where Gerda was left by the Reindeer was icy-cold and covered with snow. Her feet and hands were frozen, but she ran on bravely, towards the Palace. A flurry of snowflakes came rushing towards her. They grew bigger and bigger, until she saw that they were not snowflakes at all. They were the Snow Queen's guards - not men, but bears and snakes and porcupines, all glistening white, like the snow.

Just as poor Gerda felt she would die of cold, she suddenly found herself surrounded by a great crowd of little bright angels with spears in their hands. They struck at the Snow Queen's guards until they shattered into a thousand snowflakes. Gerda felt cold no longer. A warm glow filled her as she walked on to the palace with the angels to protect her.

Meanwhile, in the palace, Kay was playing with icicles. He often spelled whole words with them. The Snow Queen had once said to him,

"When you can form the word 'Eternity', then you shall be free."

But he never could. Although he was blue with the cold, he felt nothing. He was frozen through with the Snow Queen's enchantment, and with the splinters from the Magic Mirror. The Snow Queen had flown away that very day to touch the mountains with snow and had left Kay alone in her big Hall of Ice. This was where Gerda found him.

"Kay!" she cried in delight, running towards him. "Kay, it's your friend, Gerda. Oh, I have journeyed so far and so long to find you!"

But Kay took no notice of her at all. He stared into space with his ice cold eyes, without speaking.

Then Gerda burst into tears at his unkindness. She cried so sadly and with so much feeling, that the ice around Kay's heart began to melt, and he, too, burst into tears. A warm tear floated in his eye, and the icy splinter that had caused all the trouble so long ago, melted too.

The two friends hugged and kissed each other, and Kay's blue cheeks became fresh and glowing once more.

"Before I can be free I must do something," said Kay. "I must spell the word 'Eternity' with these icicles."

"I will help you," said Gerda.

And together they formed the one word that gave Kay his freedom. Hand in hand, they ran through the frozen palace and out into the garden where the Reindeer was waiting for them. What a journey that was! They journeyed southwards, visited the Wise Woman, and

afterwards said goodbye to the Reindeer at the home of the Lapp woman. As they wondered how they could get home without him, a horse and carriage came towards them. Gerda recognised it at once. It was the golden coach that had been given her by the Princess. And inside it was her friend, the robber girl.

Gerda greeted her as an old friend and asked her for news of everything that had happened since she had left the camp.

"Your Princess has gone travelling," said the robber girl. "And your friend the Raven is dead."

Gerda cried a little then, for the bird had been very kind to her.

"I will take you as far as the city," said the robber girl, "but then I must leave you, for I intend to travel around the world."

"No more travelling for me!" said Kay. Never again did he want to visit the northern lands or the Snow Queen. When the robber girl had dropped them off at the edge of the city, they walked hand in hand through the gates. Summer had arrived, the flowers blossomed in the gardens, and the birds sang.

And so Kay and Gerda came home again. Hardly believing her eyes, Kay's grandmother cried with joy as they came into the room. The scent of roses drifted through the window as the sun shone brightly on the happy group. And Kay forgot forever the icy kingdom of the Snow Queen where he had lived for so long.

The Robin

When up aloft
I fly and fly,
I see in pools
The shining sky,
And a happy bird
Am I, am I!

When I descend
Toward the brink
I stand and look
And stop and drink
And bathe my wings,
And chink, and prink.

When winter frost
Makes earth as steel,
I search and search
But find no meal,
And most unhappy
Then I feel.

But when it lasts,
And snows still fall,
I get to feel
No grief at all,
For I turn to a cold, stiff
Feathery ball!

Thomas Hardy

The Night Before Christmas

'Twas the night before Christmas,
When all through the house
Not a creature was stirring,
Not even a mouse;
The stockings were hung
By the chimney with care,
In hopes that St Nicholas
Soon would be there;
The children were nestled
All snug in their beds,
While visions of sugar plums
Danced in their heads.

And Mamma in her 'kerchief,
And I in my cap,
Had just settled our brains
For a long winter's nap,
When out on the lawn
There arose such a clatter,
I sprang from the bed
To see what was the matter.
Away to the window
I flew like a flash,
Tore open the shutters
And threw up the sash.

The moon, on the breast
Of the new fallen snow,
Gave the lustre of mid-day
To objects below,
When what to my wondering
Eyes should appear,
But a miniature sleigh,
And eight tiny reindeer,
With a little old driver,
So lively and quick,
I knew in a moment
It must be St Nick.

More rapid than eagles
His coursers they came,
And he whistled and shouted,
And called them by name;
"Now, Dasher! Now, Dancer!
Now, Prancer and Vixen!
On, Comet! On, Cupid!
On, Donner and Blitzen
To the top of the porch!
To the top of the wall!
Now, dash away! Dash away!
Dash away all!"

As dry leaves that before
The wild hurricane fly,
When they meet with an obstacle,
Mount to the sky;
So up to the housetop
The coursers they flew,
With the sleigh full of toys,
And St Nicholas too.

And then, in a twinkling,
I heard on the roof
The prancing and pawing
Of each little hoof –
As I drew in my head,
And was turning around,
Down the chimney St Nicholas
Came with a bound.

He was dressed all in fur,
From his head to his foot,
And his clothes were all tarnished
With ashes and soot;
A bundle of toys he had
Flung on his back,
And he looked like a pedlar
Just opening his pack.
His eyes how they twinkled!
His dimples, how merry!
His cheeks were like roses,
His nose like a cherry.

His droll little mouth
Was drawn up like a bow,
And the beard of his chin
Was as white as the snow;
The stump of his pipe he held
Tight in his teeth,
And the smoke it encircled
His head like a wreath;
He had a broad face
And a little round belly
That shook, when he laughed,
Like a bowlful of jelly.

He was chubby and plump,
A right jolly old elf,
And I laughed, when I saw him,
In spite of myself;
A wink of his eye
And a twist of his head,
Soon gave me to know
I had nothing to dread;
He spoke not a word,
But went straight to his work,
And filled all the stockings;
Then turned with a jerk,

And laying his finger
Aside of his nose,
And giving a nod,
Up the chimney he rose;
He sprang to his sleigh,
To his team gave a whistle,
And away they all flew
Like the down of a thistle.
But I heard him exclaim,
Ere he drove out of sight,
"Happy Christmas to all,
And to all a good night."

Clement C. Moore

A chapter taken from

The Wind in the Willows

by

Kenneth Grahame

Home Sweet Home

The sheep ran huddling together against the hurdles, blowing out thin nostrils and stamping with delicate fore-feet, their heads thrown back and a light steam rising from the crowded sheep-pen into the frosty air, as the two animals hastened by in high spirits, with much chatter and laughter. They were returning across country after a long day's outing with Otter, hunting and exploring on the wide uplands. The shades of the short winter day were closing in on them, and they had still some distance to go. Plodding across the field, they had heard the sheep and had made for them; and now, leading from the sheep-pen, they found a beaten track that made walking easier.

'It looks as if we are coming to a village,' said the Mole, slowing down, as the track, that had in time become a path and then had developed into a lane, now handed them over to the charge of a well metalled road. The animals did not hold with villages.

'Oh, never mind!' said the Rat. 'At this season of the year they're all safe indoors by this time, sitting round the fire; men, women, and children, dogs and cats and all. We shall slip through all right, without any bother or unpleasantness, and we can have a look at them through their windows if you like, and see what they're doing.'

The rapid nightfall of mid-December had closed in on the little village as they approached it on soft feet over a first thin fall of powdery snow. Little was visible but squares of a dusky orange-red on either side of the street, where the firelight or lamplight of each cottage overflowed through the windows into the dark world outside. Most of the low windows had no blinds, and the lookers-in from outside saw the inmates, gathered round the tea-table, absorbed in handiwork, or talking and laughing. Moving from one window to another, the two spectators, so far from home themselves, had something of wistfulness in their eyes as they watched a cat being stroked, a sleepy child picked up and huddled off to bed, or a tired man stretch and knock out his pipe on the end of a smouldering log.

Then a gust of bitter wind took them in the back of the neck, a small sting of frozen sleet on the skin woke them as from a dream, and they knew their toes to be cold and their legs tired, and their own home distant a weary way.

Once beyond the village, where the cottages ceased abruptly, on either side of the road they could smell through the darkness the friendly fields again; and they braced themselves for the last long stretch, the home stretch, the stretch that we know is bound to end, sometime, in the rattle of the door-latch, the sudden firelight, and the sight of familiar things. They plodded along steadily and silently, each of them thinking his own thoughts. The Mole's thoughts ran a good deal on supper, as it was pitch dark, and it was all a strange country to him as far as he knew, and he was following obediently behind the Rat, leaving the guidance entirely to him. As for the Rat, he was walking a little way ahead, as his habit was, his shoulders humped, his eyes fixed on the straight grey road in front of him; so he did not notice poor Mole when suddenly the call reached him, and took him like an electric shock.

It was one of these mysterious fairy calls from out of the darkness that suddenly reached Mole, making him tingle through and through with its very familiar appeal, even while as yet he could not clearly remember what it was. He stopped dead in his tracks, his nose searching hither and thither in its efforts to recapture the current that had so strongly moved him. A moment, and he had caught it again; and with it this time came recollection in fullest flood.

Home! That was what they meant, those caressing appeals, those soft touches wafted through the air, those invisible little hands pulling and tugging, all one way! Why, it must be quite close by him at that moment, his old home that he had hurriedly forsaken and never sought again, that day when he first found the river! And now it was sending out its scouts and its messengers to capture him and bring him in. Since his escape on that bright

morning he had hardly given it a thought, so absorbed had he been in his new life, in all its pleasures, its surprises, its fresh and captivating experiences. Now, with a rush of old memories, how clearly it stood up before him, in the darkness! Shabby indeed, and small and poorly furnished, and yet his, the home he had made for himself, the home he had been so happy to get back to after his day's work. And the home had been happy with him, too, and was missing him, and wanted him back, and was telling him so, through his nose.

The call was clear, the summons was plain. He must obey it instantly, and go. 'Ratty!' he called, full of joyful excitement. 'Hold on! Come back! I want you, quick!'

'Come along, Mole!' replied the Rat cheerfully, plodding along.

'Please stop, Ratty!' pleaded the poor Mole. 'You don't understand! It's my home, my old home! I've just come across the smell of it, and it's close by here, really quite close. And I must go to it, I must, I must! O, come back, Ratty! Please, please come back!'

The Rat was very far ahead, too far to hear clearly what the Mole was calling, too far to catch the sharp note of painful appeal in his voice. And he was much taken up with the weather, for he could smell something—something suspiciously like approaching snow.

'Mole, we mustn't stop now, really!' he called back. 'We'll come for it tomorrow, whatever it is you've found. But I daren't stop now—it's late, and the snow's coming on again, and I'm not sure of the way! And I want your nose, Mole, so come on quick, there's a good fellow!' The Rat pressed forward on his way without waiting for an answer.

Poor Mole stood alone in the road, his heart torn apart, and a big sob gathering, gathering, somewhere low down inside him. But even under such a test as this his loyalty to his friend stood firm. Never for a moment did he dream of abandoning him. Meanwhile, the wafts from his old home pleaded, whispered, implored, and finally claimed him. He dared not stay any longer within their magic circle. With a wrench that tore his very heart-strings he set his face down the road and followed in the track of the Rat, while faint, thin little smells, still dogging his retreating nose, reproached him for his new friendship and his cruel forgetfulness.

With an effort he caught up the unsuspecting Rat, who began chattering cheerfully about what they would do when they got back, and how fine a fire of logs in the parlour would be, and what a supper he meant to eat; never noticing his friend's silence and troubled state of mind. At last, however, when they had gone some considerable way further, and were passing some tree-stumps at the edge of a copse that bordered the road, he stopped and said kindly, 'Look here, Mole, old chap, you seem dead tired. No talk left in you, and your feet dragging like lead. We'll sit down here for a minute and rest. The snow has held off so far, and the best part of our journey is over.'

The Mole slumped on a tree-stump and tried to control himself, for he felt it surely coming. The sob he had fought with so long refused to be beaten. Up and up, it forced its way to the air, and then another, and another, and others thick and fast; till poor Mole at last gave up the struggle, and cried freely and helplessly and openly, now that he knew it was all over and he had lost what he could hardly be said to have found.

The Rat, astonished and dismayed at the Mole's grief, did not dare to speak for a while. At last he said, very quietly and sympathetically, 'What is it, old fellow? Whatever can be the matter? Tell us your trouble, and let me see what I can do.'

Poor Mole found it difficult to get any words out between the heavings of his chest that followed one upon another so quickly and held back speech and choked it as it came. 'I know it's a—shabby, dingy little place,' he sobbed at last, brokenly: 'not like—your cosy quarters—or Toad's beautiful hall—or Badger's great house—but it was my own little home—and I was fond of it—and I went away and forgot all about it—and then I smelt it suddenly—on the road, when I called and you wouldn't listen, Rat—and everything came back to me with a rush—and I wanted it!—O dear, O dear—and when you wouldn't turn back, Ratty—and I had to leave it, though I was smelling it all the time—I thought my heart would break.—We might have just gone and had one look at it, Ratty—only one look—it was close by—but you wouldn't turn back, Ratty, you wouldn't turn back! O dear, O dear!'

The memory brought fresh waves of sorrow, and sobs again took full charge of him, preventing further speech.

The Rat stared straight in front of him, saying nothing, only patting Mole gently on the shoulder. After a time he muttered gloomily, 'I see it all now! What a pig I have been! A pig—that's me! Just a pig— a plain pig!'

He waited till Mole's sobs became gradually less, till at last sniffs were frequent and sobs came only now and then. Then he rose from his seat, and, remarking carelessly, 'Well, now we'd really better be getting on, old chap!' set off up the road again, over the difficult way they had come.

'Wherever are you (hic) going to (hic), Ratty?' cried the tearful Mole, looking up in alarm.

'We're going to find that home of yours, old fellow,' replied the Rat pleasantly; 'so you had better come along, for it will take some finding, and we shall want your nose.'

'O, come back, Ratty, do!' cried the Mole, getting up and hurrying after him. 'It's no good, I tell you! It's too late, and too dark, and the place is too far off, and the snow's coming! And—and I never meant to let you know I was feeling that way about it—it was all an accident and a mistake! And think of River Bank, and your supper!'

'Hang River Bank, and supper too!' said the Rat heartily. 'I tell you, I'm going to find this place now, if I stay out all night. So cheer up, old chap, and take my arm, and we'll very soon be back there again.'

Still snuffling, pleading, and reluctant, Mole let himself be dragged back along the road by his companion. When at last it seemed to the Rat that they must be nearing that part of the road where the Mole had been 'held up', he said, 'Now, no more talking. Business! Use your nose, and give your mind to it.'

They moved on in silence for some little way, when suddenly the Rat was conscious, through his arm that was linked in Mole's, of a faint sort of electric thrill that was passing down that animal's body.

36

Instantly he disengaged himself, fell back a pace, and waited.

The signals were coming through!

Mole stood a moment rigid, while his uplifted nose, quivering slightly, felt the air.

Then a short, quick run forward—a fault—a check—a try back; and then a slow, steady, confident advance.

The Rat, much excited, kept close to his heels as the Mole, with something of the air of a sleep-walker, crossed a dry ditch, scrambled through a hedge, and nosed his way over a field open and trackless and bare in the faint starlight.

Suddenly, without giving warning, he dived; but the Rat was on the alert, and promptly followed him down the tunnel to which his nose had faithfully led him.

It was close and airless, and the earthy smell was strong, and it seemed a long time to Rat before the passage ended and he could stand up and stretch and shake himself. The Mole struck a match, and by its light the Rat saw that they were standing in an open space, neatly swept and sanded underfoot, and directly facing them was Mole's little front door, with 'Mole End' painted, in Gothic lettering, over the bell-pull at the side.

Mole reached down a lantern from a nail on the wall and lit it, and the Rat, looking round him, saw that they were in a sort of fore-court. A garden-seat stood on one side of the door, and on the other, a roller; for the Mole, who was a tidy animal when at home, could not stand having his ground kicked up by other animals into little runs that ended in earth-heaps. On the walls hung wire baskets with ferns in them, alternating with brackets carrying plaster statues. Down one side of the fore-court ran a skittle-alley, with benches along it and little wooden tables marked with rings that hinted at beer-mugs. In the middle was a round pond containing goldfish and surrounded by a cockle-shell border. Out of the centre rose a fanciful ornament clothed in more cockle-shells and topped by a large silvered glass ball that reflected everything all wrong and had a very pleasing effect.

Mole's face beamed at the sight of all these

objects so dear to him, and he hurried Rat through the door, lit a lamp in the hall, and took one glance round his old home. He saw the dust lying thick on everything, saw the cheerless, deserted look of the long-neglected house, and its modest size, its worn and shabby contents—and collapsed again on a hall-chair, his nose in his paws. 'O, Ratty!' he cried dismally, 'why ever did I do it? Why did I bring you to this poor, cold little place, on a night like this, when you might have been at River Bank by this time, toasting your toes before a blazing fire, with all your own nice things about you!'

The Rat paid no attention. He was running here and there, opening doors, inspecting rooms and cupboards, and lighting lamps and candles and sticking them up everywhere. 'What a capital little house this is!' he called out cheerily. 'So compact! So well planned! Everything here and everything in its place! We'll make a fine night of it. The first thing we want is a good fire; I'll see to that—I always know where to find things. So this is the parlour? Splendid! Your own idea, those little sleeping-bunks in the wall? Capital! Now, I'll fetch the wood and the coals, and you get a duster, Mole—you'll find one in the drawer of the kitchen table—and try and smarten things up a bit. Bustle about, old chap!'

Encouraged by his companion, the Mole roused himself and dusted and polished with energy and heartiness, while the Rat, running to and fro with armfuls of fuel, soon had a cheerful blaze roaring up the chimney. He called the Mole to come and warm himself; but Mole promptly had another fit of the blues, dropping down on a couch in dark despair and burying his face in his duster.

'Rat,' he moaned, 'how about your supper, you poor, cold, hungry, weary animal? I've nothing to give you—nothing—not a crumb!'

'What a fellow you are for giving in!' said the Rat reproachfully. 'Why, only just now I saw a sardine-opener on the kitchen dresser, quite distinctly; and everybody knows that means there are sardines about somewhere. Come on! Pull yourself together, and look around.'

So, they went hunting through every cupboard

and turned out every drawer. The result was not so very depressing after all, though of course it might have been better; a tin of sardines—a box of captain's biscuits, nearly full—and a German sausage encased in silver paper.

'There's a banquet for you!' observed the Rat, as he arranged the table. 'I know some animals who would give their ears to be sitting down to supper with us tonight!'

'No bread!' groaned the Mole; 'no butter, no—'

'No pâté de foie gras, no champagne!' continued the Rat, grinning. 'And that reminds me— what's that little door at the end of the passage? Your cellar, of course! Every luxury in this house!'

He made for the cellar door, and presently reappeared, somewhat dusty, with a bottle of beer in each paw and another under each arm. 'Self-indulgent beggar you seem to be, Mole,' he observed. 'Deny yourself nothing. This is really the nicest little place I was ever in. Now, wherever did you pick up those prints? Make the place look so home-like, they do. No wonder you're so fond of it, Mole. Tell us all about it, and how you came to make it what it is.'

Then, while the Rat busied himself fetching plates, and knives and forks, and mustard which he mixed in an egg-cup, the Mole related—somewhat shyly at first, but with more freedom as he warmed to his subject—how this was planned, and how that was thought out, and how this was got through a windfall from an aunt, and that was a wonderful find and a bargain, and this other thing was bought with hard-earned savings and a certain amount of 'going without'. His spirits finally quite restored, he had to go and touch his possessions, and take a lamp and show off their points to his visitor, and tell him all about them, quite forgetful of the supper they both so much needed; Rat, who was desperately hungry but tried to conceal it, nodded seriously, examining with a puckered brow, and saying, 'Wonderful', and 'Most remarkable', at intervals, when the chance for an observation was given him.

At last the Rat succeeded in luring him to the table, and had just got seriously to work with the sardine-opener when sounds were heard from the

40

forecourt outside—sounds like the scuffling of small feet in the gravel and a confused murmur of tiny voices, while broken sentences reached them—'Now, all in a line—hold the lantern up a bit, Tommy—clear your throats first—no coughing after I say one, two, three.—Where's young Bill?—Here, come on, do, we're all a-waiting—'

'What's up?' asked the Rat.

'I think it must be the field-mice,' replied the Mole, with a touch of pride in his manner. 'They go round carol singing regularly at this time of the year. And they never pass me over—they come to Mole End last of all; and I used to give them hot drinks, and supper too sometimes, when I could afford it. It will be like old times to hear them again.'

'Let's have a look at them!' cried the Rat, jumping up and running to the door.

It was a pretty sight that met their eyes when they flung the door open. In the forecourt, lit by the dim rays of a horn lantern, some eight or ten little field-mice stood in a semicircle, red woolly scarves round their necks, their fore-paws thrust deep into their pockets, their feet jigging for warmth. With bright eyes they glanced shyly at each other, sniggering a little, sniffing and using their coat-sleeves a good deal. As the door opened, one of the elder ones that carried the lantern was just saying, 'Now then, one, two, three!' and right away their shrill little voices arose, singing one of the old-time carols that their forefathers had composed and handed down to be sung at Yule-time.

CAROL

Villagers all, this frosty tide,
Let your doors swing open wide,
Though wind may follow, and snow beside,
Yet draw us in by your fire to bide;
    Joy shall be yours in the morning!

Here we stand in the cold and the sleet,
Blowing fingers and stamping feet,
Come from far away you to greet—
You by the fire and we in the street—
    Bidding you joy in the morning!

For ere one half of the night was gone,
Sudden a star has led us on,
Raining bliss and benison—
Bliss tomorrow and more anon,
     Joy for every morning!

Goodman Joseph toiled through the snow—
Saw the star o'er a stable low;
Mary she might not further go—
Welcome thatch, and litter below!
     Joy was hers in the morning!

And then they heard the angels tell
'Who were the first to cry Nowell?
Animals all, as it befell,
In the stable where they did dwell!
     Joy shall be theirs in the morning!'

    The voices stopped, the singers, shy but smiling, looked at each other, and silence fell but for a moment only. Then, from up above and far away, came the sound of distant bells ringing a loud and joyful peal.

    'Very well sung, boys!' cried the Rat heartily. 'And now come along in, all of you, and warm yourselves by the fire, and have something hot!'

    'Yes, come along, field-mice,' cried the Mole eagerly. 'This is quite like old times! Shut the door after you. Pull up that seat to the fire. Now, you just wait a minute, while we—O, Ratty!' he cried in despair, plumping down on a seat, close to tears. 'Whatever are we doing? We've nothing to give them!'

    'You leave all that to me,' said the masterful Rat. 'Here, you with the lantern! Come over this way. I want to talk to you. Now, tell me, are there any shops open at this hour of the night?'

    'Why, certainly, sir,' replied the field-mouse respectfully. 'At this time of the year our shops keep open to all sorts of hours.'

    'Then look here!' said the Rat. 'You go off at once, you and your lantern, and you get me—'

    Here much muttered conversation took place, and the Mole only heard bits of it, such as—'Fresh, mind!—no, a pound of that will do—see you get Buggins's, for I won't have any other—no, only the best—if you can't get it there, try somewhere else—yes, of course, home-made, no tinned stuff—well then, do the best you can!' Finally, there was a chink of coin passing from paw to paw, the field-mouse was provided with an ample basket for his purchases, and off he hurried.

The rest of the field-mice, perched in a row on the seat, their small legs swinging, gave themselves up to enjoyment of the fire, and toasted their toes till they tingled; while the Mole, failing to draw them into easy conversation, plunged into family history and made each of them recite the names of his numerous brothers, who were too young, it appeared, to be allowed to go out carolling this year.

The Rat, meanwhile, was busy examining the label on one of the beer-bottles. 'I perceive this to be Old Burton,' he remarked approvingly. 'Sensible Mole! The very thing! Now we shall be able to mull some ale! Get the things ready, Mole, while I draw the corks.'

It did not take long to prepare the brew and thrust the tin heater well into the red heart of the fire; and soon every field-mouse was sipping and coughing and choking (for a little mulled ale goes a long way) and wiping his eyes and laughing and forgetting he had ever been cold in all his life.

'They act plays too, these fellows,' the Mole explained to the Rat. 'Make them up all by them-selves, and act them afterwards. And very well they do it, too! They gave us a capital one last year, about a field-mouse who was captured at sea by a pirate, and made to row in a galley; and when he escaped and got home again, his lady-love had gone into a convent. Here, you! You were in it, I remember. Get up and recite a bit.'

The field-mouse got up on his legs, giggled shyly, looked round the room, and remained absolutely tongue-tied. His comrades cheered him on, Mole coaxed and encouraged him, and the Rat went so far as to take him by the shoulders and shake him; but nothing could overcome his stage-fright. Then the latch clicked, the door opened, and the field-mouse with the lantern reappeared, staggering under the weight of his basket.

There was no more talk of play-acting once the very real and solid contents of the basket had been tumbled out on the table. Under the generalship of Rat, everybody was set to do something or to fetch something. In a very few minutes supper was ready, and Mole, as he took the head of the table in a sort of dream, saw the board set thick with tasty treats; saw his little friends' faces brighten and beam as they fell to without delay; and then let himself loose— for he was famished indeed—on the food so magically provided, thinking what a happy home-coming this had turned out, after all. As they ate, they talked of old times, and the field-mice gave him the local gossip up to date, and answered as well as they could the hundred questions he had to ask them. The Rat said little or nothing, only taking care that each guest had what he wanted, and plenty of it, and that Mole had no trouble or worry about anything.

They clattered off at last, very grateful and showering wishes of the season, with their jacket pockets stuffed with presents for the small brothers and sisters at home. When the door had closed on the last of them and the chink of the lanterns had died away, Mole and Rat kicked the fire up, drew their chairs in, brewed themselves a last nightcap of mulled ale, and discussed the events of the long day. At last the Rat, with a tremendous yawn, said, 'Mole, old chap, I'm ready to drop. Sleepy is simply not the word. That your own bunk over on that side? Very well, then, I'll take this. What a grand little house this is! Everything so handy!'

He clambered into his bunk and rolled himself well up in the blankets, and sleep soon carried him away.

The weary Mole also was glad to turn in without delay, and soon had his head on his pillow, in great joy and contentment. But before he closed his eyes he let them wander round his old room, mellow in the glow of the firelight that played or rested on all the familiar and friendly things. He was now in just the frame of mind that the tactful Rat had quietly worked to bring about in him. He saw clearly how plain and simple—how narrow, even—it all was; but clearly, too, how much it all meant to him. He did not at all want to abandon the new life and its splendid spaces, to turn his back on sun and air and all they offered him and creep home and stay there; the upper world was all too strong, it called to him still, even down there, and he knew he must return to it. But it was good to think he had this to come back to this place which was all his own, these things which were glad to see him again and could be counted upon for the same simple welcome.

The Three Kings

Three Kings came riding from far away,
    Melchior and Gaspar and Baltasar;
Three Wise Men out of the East were they.
And they travelled by night and they slept by day,
    For their guide was a beautiful, wonderful star.

The star was so beautiful, large and clear,
    That all the other stars of the sky
Became a white mist in the atmosphere,
And by this they knew that the coming was near
    Of the Prince foretold in the prophecy.

Three caskets they bore on their saddle-bows,
    Three caskets of gold with golden keys;
Their robes were of crimson silk with rows
Of bells and pomegranates and furbelows,
    Their turbans like blossoming almond-trees.

And so the Three Kings rode into the West,
　　Through the dusk of night, over hill and dell,
And sometimes they nodded with beard on breast
And sometimes talked, as they paused to rest,
　　With the people they met at some wayside well.

'Of the child that is born,' said Baltasar,
　　'Good people, I pray you, tell us the news;
For we in the East have seen his star,
And have ridden fast, and have ridden far,
　　To find and worship the King of the Jews.'

And the people answered, 'You ask in vain;
　　We know of no king but Herod the Great!'
They thought the Wise Men were men insane,
As they spurred their horses across the plain,
　　Like riders in haste, and who cannot wait.

And when they came to Jerusalem,
      Herod the Great, who had heard this thing,
Sent for the Wise Men and questioned them;
And said, 'Go down unto Bethlehem,
      And bring me tidings of this new king.'

So they rode away; and the star stood still,
      The only one in the gray of morn;
Yes, it stopped—it stood still of its own free will,
Right over Bethlehem on the hill,
      The city of David, where Christ was born.

And the Three Kings rode through the gate and
      the guard,
      Through the silent street, till their horses turned
And neighed as they entered the great inn-yard;
But the windows were closed, and the doors
      were barred,
      And only a light in the stable burned.

And there in the scented hay,
      In the air made sweet by the breath of kine,
The little child in the manger lay,
The child, that would be king one day
      Of a kingdom not human but divine.

His mother Mary of Nazareth
    Sat watching beside his place of rest,
Watching the even flow of his breath,
For the joy of life and the terror of death
    Were mingled together in her breast.

They laid their offerings at his feet:
    The gold was their tribute to a King,
The frankincense, with its odour sweet,
Was for the Priest, the Paraclete,
    The myrrh for the body's burying.

And the mother wondered and bowed her head,
    And sat as still as a statue of stone;
Her heart was troubled yet comforted,
Remembering what the Angel had said
    Of an endless reign and of David's throne.

Then the Kings rode out of the city gate,
    With a clatter of hoofs in proud array;
But they went not back to Herod the Great,
For they knew his malice and feared his hate,
    And returned to their homes by another way.

Henry Wadsworth Longfellow

49

The Little Match Girl

It was terribly cold. The snow fell, covering the roads and roofs of the big city. It was New Year's Eve, the very last night of the year. Inside the big houses, people were eating, drinking and dancing, while under glittering Christmas trees, all covered with candles, the children played.

Outside in the snowy street, a little girl was hurrying along. She had a thin, ragged cloak and bare, frozen feet. When she had left home that morning, she had worn a pair of slippers. They were too big for her and had fallen off and been lost during the day. She carried with her a small bundle of matches, for she was a Match Girl who sold them for a living. That day she had been very unlucky. She had not sold one match or earned any money at all. People had been too busy hurrying home in the snow to the warmth and comfort of their homes, to spare a thought for the little, frozen, starving girl.

She was a pretty child with long, golden hair. Her little body was painfully thin; and her cheeks, usually pale and pinched, were now red with the cold. As she hurried along, she saw through every window the lights of candles and lamps and the warm glow from countless stoves. In some windows she saw people laughing and talking. In others she saw tables all set with more food than she had eaten in her entire life.

The Little Match Girl's mouth watered as she imagined the smell of the roast meat, the warm, thick soup and the spicy puddings.

Very soon, the Little Match Girl's footsteps grew slower and slower until at last she stopped altogether and huddled in a corner between two houses. It was not just the cold that made her stop here. She knew she would be in trouble when she reached the attic that was home. For when her father knew that she had sold no matches, he would beat her.

'The matches!' she thought. 'Perhaps the light from their flames will warm me.' So the Little Match Girl lit one match and held her hands over the warm glow. She sighed happily as the match began to warm her hands. The bright, flickering light made it seem that she was no longer crouched in her dark, cold corner. Instead, she was sitting beside a large stove that glowed with warmth and comfort.

"How wonderful it feels!" she said, and she stretched out her poor, frozen feet to warm them. But before she could do so, the flame died away, and the stove vanished. Once more she found herself on the pavement, leaning against the cold stone of the house.

'Perhaps if I light another match, I will see the stove again,' she thought. When she did so, she found she could see right through the walls of the house into the room behind it. There was a long table there,

51

covered with a white cloth with plate after plate of mouth watering food. There was a huge joint of roast turkey, and it seemed to the Little Match Girl that she was near enough to carve herself a thick slice of it. But even as she reached out to take a knife, the match burnt down and the flame died. Instead of the festive room, the Little Match Girl was once again outside in the snowy street, crouched against the hard, stone wall.

Her fingers were so frozen that she could scarcely move them to light the third match, but at last she managed it. How glad she was that she did so. Now she was sitting under a beautiful Christmas tree that was ablaze with a hundred candles. Glass balls and little wooden angels hung from its branches. The Little Match Girl had never seen anything so wonderful in her life. At home there was only a single candle to light the little, bare attic room. The Little Match Girl stared and stared. She did not notice the match go out. The tree did not fade away as everything had done before. The lights on the branches flared higher and higher, and one fell down from the top of the tree.

"It looks exactly like a falling star," said the Little Match Girl. "My grandmother always said that a falling star means that someone has died." Her eyes filled with tears as she remembered her grandmother. She had been the only person who had ever loved her, and now she was dead.

The Christmas tree faded and the Little Match Girl lit a fourth match. She gave a cry, for there in front of her was the one person she thought she would never see again.

"Grandmother!" she cried. "You have come back to me! Oh, I must quickly light the other matches or else you will fade away."

Fumbling in her bundle with her numb, cold fingers, the Little Match Girl lit all of the remaining matches. The light from them shone into her cold corner and stretched out into the snowy, cold streets of the city. The Little Match Girl shielded her eyes from the brilliant light and looked up. Her grandmother still stood there and she seemed to grow taller and taller. Her face shone with beauty and kindness. She stooped

down and took the Little Match Girl's cold hands in her own. Then she gathered her up in her arms and flew with her over the city, just as the bells from all the churches rang in the New Year.

They flew higher and higher until the coldness of this world gave way to the brilliance of Paradise.

The next morning, the people from the house where the Little Match Girl had found shelter looked out of their door.

"Oh dear, how sad!" they cried. "There's a little girl out here. She must have frozen to death."

For the Little Match Girl lay there. She did not look dead, for her cheeks were glowing and there was a happy smile on her face. But she had died with the Old Year at midnight. Around her lay a pile of spent matches.

"Oh look, she tried to warm herself to keep alive," said the lady of the house. "Poor little thing. And so beautiful, too!"

Not one of them knew of the wonderful things the Little Match Girl had seen in the last hours of her life. And they did not know that now, up in Heaven, she was celebrating the best New Year ever with her beloved grandmother.

The North Wind Doth Blow

The north wind doth blow,
And we shall have snow,
And what will the robin do then, poor thing?
    He'll sit in a barn,
    And keep himself warm,
And hide his head under his wing, poor thing!

The north wind doth blow,
And we shall have snow,
And what will the swallow do then, poor thing?
    Oh, do you not know
    That he's off long ago,
To a country where he will find spring, poor thing!

The north wind doth blow,
And we shall have snow,
And what will the dormouse do then, poor thing?
    Roll'd up like a ball,
    In his nest snug and small,
He'll sleep till warm weather comes in, poor thing!

The north wind doth blow,
And we shall have snow,
And what will the honey-bee do then, poor thing?
    In his hive he will stay
    Till the cold is away,
And then he'll come out in the spring, poor thing!

The north wind doth blow,
And we shall have snow,
And what will the children do then, poor things?
    When lessons are done,
    They must skip, jump and run,
Until they have made themselves warm, poor things!

Anonymous

A Christmas Carol

by Charles Dickens

Adapted by Gill Davies

Illustrated by Eric Kincaid

Introduction

Charles Dickens' *A Christmas Carol* was first published in 1852, and has since become one of the best-loved tales of Christmas. Dickens tells the story of Ebenezer Scrooge, a cold, miserly character who is avoided by all apart from his warm-hearted nephew. Scrooge spends his days making money, and his evenings counting all that he has made. So it comes as no surprise that Scrooge chooses not to celebrate Christmas, thinking it extremely extravagant and a complete waste of time.

However, on one particular Christmas Eve, the haunting of Ebenezer Scrooge begins. He is visited by three Spirits and each in turn reveal to Scrooge how lacking he is in warmth and compassion. During these visitations Dickens introduces the reader to a wealth of vital characters; Bob Cratchit and his family, especially Tiny Tim, whose strength and courage help Scrooge realize the error of his ways, and Scrooge's nephew, whose offer of friendship Scrooge finally accepts. Throughout the story there prevails an atmosphere of festive cheer as people forget their grievances at Christmas time.

A Christmas Carol is the perfect blend of comedy and horror. Highly acclaimed children's artist Eric Kincaid graphically evokes the squalor of Victorian London, the horror of the ghostly apparitions and the joy of Christmas.

Chapter One

Marley's Ghost

Marley was dead: to begin with. There is no doubt whatever about that. The register of his burial was signed by the clergyman, the clerk, the undertaker – and his chief mourner and business partner of many a year – Scrooge. Old Marley was dead, dead as a doornail.

Scrooge never painted out Old Marley's name. There it stood, years afterwards, above the warehouse door: Scrooge and Marley. Sometimes people called Scrooge Scrooge, and sometimes Marley, but it was all the same to him.

Oh, but he was a tight-fisted hand at the grindstone, Scrooge! A squeezing, wrenching, scraping, clutching, jealous old sinner! Hard and sharp as flint, and solitary as an oyster in his shell. The cold within

57

him froze his old features, nipped his pointed nose, shrivelled his cheek, sharpened his grating voice, made his eyes red and his thin lips blue. There was a cold frosty rim to his head, his eyebrows and his wiry chin. Scrooge carried his own low temperature about with him; he iced his office and he didn't thaw it one degree at Christmas.

No wind that blew was bitterer than Scrooge, no winter snow was more intent upon its falling, no pelting rain more likely to pause when begged to do so.

Nobody ever stopped him in the street to say, with welcoming looks, "My dear Scrooge, how are you? When will you come to see me?" No beggars implored him for a trifle, no children asked him what it was o'clock, no-one ever once inquired the way to such and such, of Scrooge. Even blind men's dogs would tug their owners into doorways when they saw Scrooge coming, wagging their tails as if to say, "No eye at all is better than an evil eye!"

But what did Scrooge care! This was the very thing he liked, to edge his way along the crowded paths of life, warning everyone to keep their distance.

Once upon a time, on Christmas Eve, old Scrooge sat busy in his counting house. It was cold, bleak, biting weather: and foggy. Scrooge could hear the people go wheezing up and down outside, beating their hands upon their breasts, stamping to warm their feet. The city clocks had only just gone three but it was dark already; candles flared in the windows. The fog was dense. It came pouring in at every chink

58

and keyhole and, although the courtyard outside was narrow, the houses opposite were mere phantoms.

The door of Scrooge's counting house was open so that he might keep his eye upon his clerk who, in a dismal little cell beyond, was copying letters. Scrooge had a very small fire but the clerk's was so mean that it looked like just one coal. The fuel was kept in Scrooge's room and the clerk did not dare to replenish his meagre fire. So poor frozen Bob Cratchit put on his white comforter and tried to warm his hands at the candle instead!

"A merry Christmas, Uncle! God save you!" cried a cheerful voice. The voice belonged to Scrooge's nephew, Fred, who was all aglow from walking in the cold.

"Bah!" said Scrooge. "Humbug!"

"Christmas a humbug, Uncle!" cried Fred. "You don't mean that, I am sure?"

"I do," said Scrooge. "What right have you to be merry? You're poor enough. And have a young wife to support, moreover. If there is any one thing more ridiculous than a merry Christmas, it is falling in love. Bah! What's Christmas to you, anyway, but a time for paying bills without money!"

"If I had my way," continued Scrooge. "Every idiot who goes about with 'Merry Christmas' on his lips should be boiled with his pudding and buried with a stick of holly through his heart!"

"Oh Uncle," cried his nephew Fred, "I cannot claim that Christmas has ever put gold or silver in my pocket but it *has* done me good and *will* do me good and I say, God Bless it!"

The clerk could not help but applaud.

"Let me hear another sound from you," cried Scrooge, "and you will celebrate Christmas by losing your job."

"Don't be angry, Uncle," begged Fred. "Come! Dine with us tomorrow."

"Nephew," said Scrooge, "you keep Christmas in your way and let me keep it in mine. Good afternoon!"

"But you don't keep it all," said Fred sadly. "I am sorry with all my heart, Uncle, to find you so. Well, a Happy New Year then!"

"Good afternoon!" said Scrooge, dismissing his disappointed nephew just as two portly gentlemen swept inside.

"Have I the pleasure of addressing Mr Scrooge or Mr Marley?" inquired one.

"Marley," Scrooge grunted, "died seven years ago, this very night."

"No doubt his generosity is shared by his surviving partner." (This was true enough: for each partner had been as mean as the other.) "A few of us are trying," went on the gentleman, "to raise a fund to buy the poor some meat and drink, and the means of warmth. What shall I put you down for?"

"Nothing!" snapped Scrooge. "Are there no prisons?"

"Plenty," answered the gentleman.

"And workhouses?" asked Scrooge.

"Both are very busy," returned the gentleman. "And many would rather die than go there."

"Then they had better do it," said Scrooge, "and decrease the surplus population. Good afternoon."

Scrooge returned to his paperwork, pleased at his wit. Outside the cold, the dark and the fog grew even denser.

"God bless you merry gentleman…"

The voice of a caroller rang at the keyhole but as Scrooge seized his ruler the singer fled in terror.

At length it was time to shut up the counting house. The clerk snuffed out his candle.

"You will want all day off tomorrow, I suppose?" asked Scrooge.

"If quite convenient, sir."

"It is not convenient, or fair," grumbled Scrooge. "Be sure to be here all the earlier the next morning," he added with a growl. Then Bob Cratchit, in happy release from his cold cell, joined a line of merry boys for a slide on the ice before running home to his family.

Scrooge took a melancholy dinner in a melancholy tavern and then went back to his gloomy chambers. The courtyard was dark. Scrooge had to grope along to find where to put his key. It was then that he saw the knocker: but now it was not a knocker at all. It was Marley's face.

It stared at Scrooge, its hair stirring and its eyes wide open. It was horrible. Up the dark stairs went Scrooge and looked all about to make sure there were no other unpleasant surprises. There was nobody, not even in his dressing gown although this was hanging in a suspicious way against the wall.

"Humbug!" said Scrooge, undressing and sitting beside the fire to take his gruel. But then the bell began to swing eerily.

Soon it was ringing loudly, along with every other bell in the house. And as that dreadful din died away, it was followed by the noise of dragging chains.

The chains clanked their way upstairs and in through the heavy door.

"Marley's ghost!" cried Scrooge. So it was, Marley, all wrapped about with great coils of cash boxes, keys, padlocks, ledgers, deeds and heavy purses wrought in steel.

"What do you want with me?" gasped Scrooge.

"Much!" said the voice of Marley.

"Bah!" said Scrooge. "My stomach affects my senses. You may be an indigested bit of beef or a blob of mustard. There is more of gravy about you than the grave. Humbug, I tell you – humbug!"

At this, the spirit raised a frightful cry, wrung its shadowy hands and shook its chain. This made such an appalling noise that Scrooge fell upon his knees, crying, "Why are you so fettered?"

"I wear the chain I forged in life, link by link, of my own free will. But the length of the chain you bear, Scrooge, is greater still. It is a ponderous heavy chain. Hear me! My time is nearly gone. You will be haunted by three ghosts, the first at one o'clock. Through them, you may yet have a chance to escape my fate. Remember me!"

The ghost floated back as the window raised itself. Outside, the air was filled with chained, moaning phantoms, full of eternal misery. As Scrooge stared, the miserable wretches faded into mist.

Exhausted, he dropped onto his bed and fell instantly asleep.

Chapter Two

The First of the Three Spirits

When Scrooge awoke, it was dark. The chimes of a neighbouring clock struck twelve. Scrooge was astonished. It had been past two when he went to bed. An icicle must have jammed the clock works.

"Or have I slept through a whole day?" Scrooge wondered. He scrambled out of bed and groped to the window but all that he could make out was that it was still foggy and extremely cold. Scrooge slid back into his bed. Had Marley been a dream or not? Would the three ghosts come as promised? Would the first arrive when the bell tolled one?

Ding, dong!

"A quarter past!" said Scrooge.

Ding, dong!

"Half past!" said Scrooge.

Ding, dong!

"A quarter to it!" said Scrooge.

Ding, dong!

"The hour itself!" said Scrooge. Then, as the bell sounded its final melancholy chime, lights flashed into his room and a hand drew back the curtains of his bed.

Scrooge found himself staring at a strange figure. It seemed like a child, with a tender bloom upon the skin and yet it looked like an old man too, with hair white as if with age. The Ghost carried a branch of holly and wore a lustrous belt. From its head sprang a jet of clear light and it carried a great cap under its arm. The figure seemed to change all the time,

dissolving in and out of light and dark.

"I am the Ghost of Christmas Past," said a gentle voice. "Rise and walk with me."

It would have been in vain for Scrooge to mention the hour, that his bed was warm and the weather freezing, that he was clad in just slippers and dressing gown. The Spirit's grasp was firm. He drew Scrooge with him, out through the window. The city, and the darkness, vanished. They stood upon an open country road.

"Goodness!" said Scrooge, recognising every gate and tree, and the children playing in the fields. "I was a boy here."

"These are but shadows of things that have been," explained the Ghost. "They are not aware of us, not even this unhappy little child."

There in the school sat the young Ebenezer Scrooge as was, alone and friendless. The memory of his boyhood made Scrooge sob and then, with a pang, Scrooge recalled the young carol singing lad he had so fiercely chased away.

On they went to visit other Christmases; to see Scrooge's sister Fan, mother of Scrooge's nephew Fred – so sweet and affectionate in her youth before her untimely death.

Then on they travelled through time to see the Fezziwigs, Scrooge's first employers, dancing and feasting to celebrate Christmas Eve, their generosity and merry spirits such a contrast to Scrooge's miserable treatment of his own clerk. Fuel was heaped upon the fire, the warehouse was snug and warm and dry

as the beaming loveable Fezziwigs turned it into a bright ballroom.

On again – next to see Belle, that enchanting fair girl who had loved the young Ebenezer well until his lust for money had displaced his love for her.

Here was Belle now making that painful parting from Young Ebenezer Scrooge, her eyes brimming with tears:

"Our contract is an old one, made when we were poor and content to be so. I release you, with a full heart. And I know that whatever pain there is, you will soon dismiss the memory of it – as an unprofitable dream."

And now here was Belle again, much later on, grown to be a comely matron, her family and grandchildren all around her, bubbling with merriment. But then the family conversation turned to Scrooge still busy in his office, ignoring his partner, Marley, left alone upon the point of death that very Christmas Eve.

"Show me no more!" cried Scrooge. "Take me home. I cannot bear it!"

In desperation Scrooge tried to quench the Spirit's light. He seized his great candle snuffer of a cap and plunged it over him but still the Spirit's light poured out.

Scrooge was conscious of being suddenly quite exhausted. But then, all at once, he found himself back in his own room. He barely had time to reel into bed before sinking into a heavy sleep.

Chapter Three

The Second of the Three Spirits

It was a violent snore that woke him but
Scrooge realised that once again the bell
was tolling one. He waited…Nothing
happened until he became aware of a blaze
of ruddy light coming from the adjoining
room. Rather nervously, Scrooge arose and
shuffled in his slippers to the door.

What a sight met his eyes. His room
was hung with living green, like a perfect
grove where holly, ivy, mistletoe and bright
berries glistened. A mighty blaze was
roaring up the chimney.

"Come in," called a jovial voice.
"Come in! And know me better."

There – on a throne of turkeys, geese,
poultry, joints of meat, sucking pigs,
sausages, plum puddings, mince pies,
barrels of oysters, red-hot chestnuts, cherry-
cheeked apples, luscious oranges and pears,
immense twelfth cakes and seething bowls
of punch – sat a glorious giant. He wore a
dark green mantle trimmed with fur and an
antique scabbard at his waist. The Spirit
was holding high a glowing torch like
Plenty's horn.

Scrooge entered timidly. He had
learned to be ashamed of his past doings
now and hung his head: the Spirit's eyes
were clear and kind but Scrooge was afraid
to meet them.

"I am the Ghost of Christmas
Present," announced the cheery Spirit.
"Look upon me!"

He had long dark brown curls on

which sat a holly wreath scattered with shining icicles.

"You have never seen the like of me before!" exclaimed the Spirit.

"Never," said Scrooge.

The Ghost of Christmas Present rose.

"Spirit," said Scrooge submissively, "conduct me where you will. I learnt a lesson last night. Tonight, if you have anything to teach me, let me profit by it."

"Touch my robe," instructed the Spirit.

Scrooge did as he was told and held it fast. In an instant, the green grove, the holly and berries, the heaped banquet of festive fare, the roaring fire and the deep hour of night were gone.

They stood in the city streets on Christmas morning. People made a rough brisk kind of music, scraping the snow from the pavements in front of their dwellings and from the tops of their houses so that it came plumping down into the road below – or fell in flurries like miniature snow storms – to the mad delight of the little boys beneath.

The house fronts looked black and the windows blacker against the white sheet of snow upon the roofs. On the roads, the heavy wheels of carts and wagons had made icy furrows that crossed and recrossed each other hundreds of times in the thick yellow mud and icy water.

The sky was gloomy and the smaller streets choked with mist but the people shovelling snow on the rooftops were jovial and full of glee, calling out to each other from the parapets, hurling the odd

snowball and laughing heartily.

The poulterers' shops were still open. And the fruiterers were radiant in their glory. Onions shone in the fatness of their growth like Spanish friars, pears and apples clustered high in blooming pyramids, the juiciest oranges and lemons entreated to be carried home in paper bags.

And the Grocers! Oh, the Grocers! The almonds so extremely white, the cinnamon sticks so long and straight, the figs so moist and the French plums blushing in highly decorated boxes. Customers tumbled up against each other and clashed their wicker baskets wildly, so hurried and eager in the hopeful promise of the day.

But soon the steeples called good people all to church and chapel, flocking through the streets in their best clothes, while the poorer folk carried their dinners to the bakers to cook. As these revellers passed, the Spirit sprinkled drops of water and incense from his torch onto the revellers and onto their dinners. As he did so any angry words, as they jostled each other, instantly dispersed and all agreed it was a shame to quarrel on Christmas Day.

"Is there a special flavour that you sprinkle from your torch?" asked Scrooge.

"There is. My own!" answered the Spirit.

"Would it apply to any kind of dinner on this day?" asked Scrooge.

"To any kindly given. To a poor one most."

On went Scrooge and the Ghost of Christmas Present, invisible as before, Scrooge still holding onto the Spirit's robe, into the suburbs of the town until at last they arrived at the dwelling of Bob Cratchit, Scrooge's clerk. Whereupon, on the threshold of the door, the Spirit smiled and stopped to bless this poor home too with the sprinkling of his torch.

Then up rose Mrs Cratchit, brave in bright cheap ribbons on her twice-turned gown to lay the table helped by her daughter Belinda, while young Master Peter plunged a fork into the saucepan of potatoes.

And now the two smaller Cratchits, boy and girl, came tearing in, screaming that outside the bakers they had smelt the goose and known it for their own. Basking in luxurious thoughts of sage and onion, these young Cratchits danced about the table while Peter Cratchit blew the fire until the potatoes bubbled up, knocking loudly at the saucepan lid to be let out and peeled.

"Whatever has got your precious father then?" said Mrs Cratchit. "And your brother Tiny Tim; and Martha warn't as late last Christmas Day by half an hour!"

"Here's Martha, mother!" announced a young girl, appearing as she spoke.

"It's Martha!" cried the two young Cratchits. "Hurrah! There's such a goose, Martha."

"Why bless your heart alive, my dear, how late you are!" cried Mrs Cratchit, kissing Martha a dozen times and taking off her shawl and bonnet for her.

"We'd a deal of work to finish last night, and then we had to clear away this morning," explained her daughter.

"Well, never mind, so long as you are

come," said Mrs Cratchit. "Sit ye down before the fire, my dear."

"No! Quick, hide. There's father coming!" cried the two young Cratchits, who were everywhere at once. "Hide, Martha, hide!"

So Martha hid herself as in came Bob Cratchit with at least three feet of comforter hanging down before him and his threadbare clothes darned up and brushed to look seasonable; and Tiny Tim upon his shoulder. Alas for Tiny Tim, he bore a little crutch and had his limbs supported by an iron frame.

"Why, where's our Martha?" asked Bob Cratchit looking all around.

"Not coming!" answered Mrs Cratchit.

"Not coming!" cried Bob. "Not coming on Christmas Day!" his rampant high spirits tumbling in his sudden disappointment. At which point, Martha could bear it no longer, even if it was only a joke. She came running out from behind the closet straight into her father's arms while the two young Cratchits hustled Tiny Tim and bore him off into the wash-house so that he might hear the pudding singing in the copper.

"And how did little Tim behave?" asked Mrs Cratchit as Bob hugged his daughter to his heart's content.

"As good as gold," said Bob, his voice trembling, "and better. I suppose, he gets thoughtful sitting by himself so much and thinks the strangest things. He told me coming home that he hoped the people saw him in the church, because he was a cripple, and it might be pleasant for them to remember on Christmas Day who it was that made lame beggars walk and blind men see."

Then back came Tiny Tim to sit upon his stool by the fire while Bob put a jug of gin and lemons on the hob to simmer and the young Cratchits fetched the goose. Mrs Cratchit made the gravy hissing hot, Master Peter mashed the potatoes with incredible vigour, and Miss Belinda sweetened up the apple sauce. Then at last the two young Cratchits returned in high procession with the goose. They set out all the chairs, the young ones cramming spoons into their mouths lest they shriek for goose before their turn to be helped came.

Grace was said. There was a breathless pause – then Mrs Cratchit plunged the carving knife into the breast. There was a sudden gush of stuffing and a murmur of delight from all around. Oh, there never was such a goose! Bob Cratchit said he didn't believe there ever was such a goose cooked! Its tenderness, size, flavour, and cheapness were the subject of wild admiration.

And, oh, what a wonderful pudding! Hard and firm like a speckled cannon-ball, blazing in half a quartern of lit brandy and crowned with holly. Bob said it was the greatest success achieved by Mrs Cratchit since their marriage.

At last the dinner was done, the hearth swept and the fire made up. Apples and oranges were put upon the table and a shovel-full of chestnuts on the fire. Then the family drew around the hearth as, with

beaming looks, Bob served out the hot stuff from the jug while the chestnuts on the fire sputtered and crackled noisily.

Then Bob proposed:

"A Merry Christmas to us all, my dears. God bless us." Which all the family re-echoed.

"God bless us every one!" cried Tiny Tim, the last of all.

He sat very close to his father's side, upon his little stool. Bob held his withered little hand in his as if he loved the child and wished to keep him by his side, and dreaded that he might be taken from him.

"Spirit," asked Scrooge, with an interest he had never felt before. "Tell me if Tiny Tim will live."

"I see a vacant seat," replied the Ghost, "in the poor chimney corner, and a crutch without an owner, carefully preserved. If these shadows remain unaltered by the Future, the child will die."

"No, no," said Scrooge. "Oh no, kind Spirit! Say he will be spared."

"If these shadows remain unaltered by the Future," repeated the Ghost, "none other of my race will find him here. What then? If he be like to die, he had better do it, and decrease the surplus population."

Scrooge hung his head to hear his own words quoted so. He bent before the Ghost's anger, quite overcome with guilt and grief. Trembling, he cast his eyes upon the ground but raised them speedily upon hearing his own name.

"Mr Scrooge!" said Bob. "I'll give you Mr Scrooge, the founder of the Feast."

"Founder of the Feast indeed!" cried

Mrs Cratchit. "I wish I had him here. I'd give him a piece of my mind to feast upon!"

"My dear," protested Bob, "the children! Christmas Day."

"It would have to be Christmas day, I am sure, to drink the health of such an odious, stingy, hard, unfeeling man. I'll drink his health for your sake and the Day's," said Mrs Cratchit, "but not for his. Long life to him. A Merry Christmas and a Happy New Year."

The children drank the toast after her but there was no heartiness in it. Tiny Tim didn't care tuppence for it. Scrooge was the ogre of the family and the mention of his name had cast a dark shadow on the party.

But after this had passed they were all ten times merrier than before from the sheer relief of being done with Scrooge the Baleful!

Bob told them he was sorting out a job for Master Peter who looked thoughtfully into the fire while the little ones laughed to think of their brother as a man of business. It would bring in a full five-and-sixpence weekly, explained Bob. Then it was Martha's turn to tell them all about her work as a milliner's apprentice. And all this time the chestnuts and the jug went round. Bye and bye Tiny Tim sang a song about a lost child travelling in the snow. He had such a sweet, plaintive, little voice and sang it very well indeed.

This was not a particularly handsome family. They were not well dressed and their shoes were far from waterproof but they were happy, grateful and pleased with

one another.

By now it was getting dark and snowing heavily. The Cratchit family looked happier yet in the bright sprinklings from the Spirit's torch but then they all faded away from Scrooge's gaze as he and the Spirit once again set off into the evening.

Everywhere, friends and families met merrily at doorways as the indoor glow spilled out into the dark and, ahead, the lamplighter ran on, dotting the dusky streets with specks of light.

Together Scrooge and Spirit moved away from the snowbound city out onto bleak desert moors where miners lived, to bless their poor houses too – and then across black and heaving seas to spread the Christmas spirit onto lighthouse and ship where men still made merry amid the awful icy waves.

At last they found themselves back in a bright gleaming room. It was with sudden surprise that Scrooge recognised this as his own nephew's. A party of some twenty people, young and old, was in full sway and everyone was laughing.

"Ha, ha, ha, ha, ha! He said that Christmas was a humbug, as I live!" roared Scrooge's nephew, Fred.

"More shame for him!" cried Scrooge's pretty niece by marriage.

"I am sorry for him," said Fred. "He's a comical old fellow and I couldn't be angry with him if I tried. Who suffers by his ill whims? Himself, always."

After tea, the party turned to music, and then to games of Blind Man's Buff and

Forfeits and How.

Scrooge found himself caught up in the infectious fun of it all, guessing at the answers and forgetting that his voice made no sound in their ears.

The Ghost was greatly pleased to find Scrooge in this mood. Scrooge was begging now to stay longer as a new game called Yes and No began, a guessing game.

A brisk fire of questioning established that Scrooge's nephew had chosen to think of an animal, a rather disagreeable animal, a savage animal that growled and grunted and walked the London streets. Yes, it talked sometimes. No, it didn't live in a zoo, it was never taken to market. It wasn't a horse, a donkey, a cow, a pig, a dog, a tiger or a bear.

At last the plump sister of Scrooge's niece cried out, "I have found it out! I know what it is, Fred, I know."

"What is it?" asked Fred.

"It's your Uncle Scro-o-o-o-oge!"

Which it certainly was. Several felt that the reply to "Is it a bear?" ought to have been "Yes" but all agreed that Uncle Scrooge had certainly given them a plenty of merriment tonight.

"A Merry Christmas and a Happy New Year to the old man, whatever he is!" said Scrooge's nephew. "He wouldn't take it from me but he may have it, nevertheless. Uncle Scrooge!"

Scrooge had become so merry he would have toasted the company in return but now the whole scene passed off in the breath of the last word spoken by his nephew.

Once again the Spirit took Scrooge away with him upon his travels. Much they saw, and far they went. The Spirit stood beside the ill and the homesick; he went into almshouse, hospital and jail – and, everywhere, he left his blessing and made folk cheerful.

It was a long night – if it were only a night, for time seemed compressed and soon it was Twelfth Night. The Ghost appeared to have grown much older, and his hair had turned from brown to grey.

"Are spirits' lives so short?" asked Scrooge.

"My life upon this globe is very brief," replied the Ghost. "It ends tonight, at midnight."

Already the chimes were ringing three quarters past eleven. It was then that Scrooge noticed two wretched children kneeling at the Spirit's feet. Yellow, ragged, scowling and wolfish they were, bowed down and looking as if a shrivelled hand had pinched and twisted them, and torn them into shreds.

"Spirit," asked Scrooge, appalled by the sight of the pitiful creatures clinging to the Spirit for protection, "are they yours?"

"They are Man's," said the Spirit. "This boy is Ignorance. This girl is Want. Beware them both."

"Have they no refuge or resource?" cried Scrooge.

"Are there no prisons? Are there no workhouses?" retorted the Spirit. But just then the clock struck twelve – and with the final chime, the Ghost of Christmas Present vanished.

Chapter Four

The Last of the Spirits

Now, to take the place of the second ghost, arrived the third and final spirit. This was a solemn phantom, draped and hooded, and coming towards Scrooge like a mist along the ground. Slowly, gravely, silently, the phantom approached until at last the tall stately form came close. Scrooge dropped onto his knees for, as it moved, this Spirit seemed to scatter gloom and mystery.

It was difficult to separate the figure from the darkness, to shape it from the night. It was shrouded in a long dark garment which concealed its face and form, save for one outstretched hand.

"Am I in the presence of the Ghost of Christmas Yet to Come?" inquired Scrooge.

The Spirit answered not but its spectral hand pointed onwards. Scrooge was filled with a vague uncertain horror to know that behind the dusky shroud there were ghostly eyes intently fixed upon him. His legs trembled so much that he could scarcely stand to follow as he cried, "Ghost of the Future, I fear you more than any spectre I have seen. But I know your purpose is to do me good. Lead on, Spirit!"

Then Scrooge found himself born up in the shadow of the Spirit's robe and the city seemed to spring up about them.

Here were knots of business men and merchants, clinking the money in their pockets and conversing. The Spirit stopped beside one group, pointing its spectral hand. Scrooge stepped forward to listen.

"When did he die?" one was asking.

"Last night I believe."

"What has he done with all his money?" inquired a red-nosed gentleman.

"Left it to his Company, perhaps. He hasn't left it to me. That's all I know." Amid general laughter the man went on to suggest it would be a very cheap funeral, "For upon my life, I don't know of anybody to go to it. Suppose we make up a party and volunteer?"

As the group broke up, still laughing, the Phantom glided into a street where stood two business acquaintances of Scrooge, men whom Scrooge had often sought to impress.

"Well," said one. "Old Scratch has got his own at last, hey?"

"So I am told," replied the other and then went on to talk about more meaningful matters such as the weather.

Scrooge wondered why the Spirit thought these scraps of conversation important. He looked about in his usual

places for any signs of his own future self here but there was none. Still the Spirit stood in silence beside him with its outstretched hand and those unseen eyes that observed him keenly. It made Scrooge shudder and feel very cold.

They left the busy scene now and went into an obscure part of town. The ways were foul and narrow, the shops and houses wretched, the people half-naked, drunken, slipshod. Alleys and archways spilled smells and dirt into the straggling streets and the whole quarter reeked with crime, filth and misery.

Here, upon the floor of a low-roofed shop, amongst mountains of unseemly old rags, bottles, bones, greasy offal, nails, rusty keys, chains and refuse iron of all kinds, sat Old Joe. Screened from the cold air by the tattered shreds of a curtain and huddled close to a charcoal stove, the grey-haired old rascal was smoking his pipe.

Just as Scrooge and the Phantom slipped inside, a woman with a heavy bundle slunk into the shop. Then came another woman, similarly laden, and then a man in faded black. Each recognised the others. There was a short period of blank astonishment and then all three burst into laughter.

"Let the charwoman be first, let the laundress be second and let the undertaker's man be third!" cried the first woman. "Look here, Old Joe, what a chance, we three all meeting here without meaning it."

"You couldn't have met in a better place," croaked Old Joe. "Now come into the parlour, come, come!"

The parlour was the space behind the screen of rags. The old man raked the fire with an old stair rod and trimmed a smoky lamp before putting the stem of his pipe back into his mouth.

By now the charwoman had thrown down her bundle and sat upon a stool.

"Why then, don't stand staring as if you was afraid," she jeered. "Who's the worse for a loss of a few things like these? Not a dead man, I suppose."

"No, indeed!" screeched Mrs Dibner, laughing.

"Wicked old screw," said the woman. "Why wasn't he natural in his lifetime, then he'd have had someone to look after him instead of gasping out his last on his own!"

One by one, the bundles were opened. Inside the undertaker man's was a seal or two, a pencil case, buttons and a brooch. Mrs Dibner's contained some sheets, towels, clothing, boots, teaspoons and a pair of sugar tongues.

"Now undo my bundle," said the first woman. "I wish it were a heavier one." Joe dragged out a large roll of bedcurtains.

"You don't mean to say you took 'em down, rings and all, with him lying there?" asked Joe

"Yes, I do. Why not?"

"You were born to make your fortune," said Joe, unravelling blankets too.

"I shouldn't hold my hand back for the sake of such a man as he was," said the woman. "He isn't likely to catch cold without 'em, now eh?"

Scrooge watched in horror as the dead

man's best fine shirt appeared.

"They'd have wasted it otherwise," explained the woman. "They'd put it on him to be buried in but I took it off again. Calico's good enough. He can't look uglier in that than he did in this one."

The four figures sat grouped about their spoil in the scanty light of the old man's lamp like horrid demons as the woman cackled, "This is the end of it, you see. He frightened every one away from him when he was alive, to profit us when he was dead. Ha, ha, ha!"

"Spirit," said Scrooge, shuddering from head to foot, "The case of this unhappy man might be my own. My life leads that way, now. Merciful Heaven, what is this?"

Scrooge recoiled in terror for the scene had changed and now he almost touched a bed, a bare uncurtained bed where something lay beneath a ragged sheet, covered up – dumb, no longer able to speak, but announcing its presence in this awful show of death.

The room was very dark. But as Scrooge glanced towards the Phantom a pale light fell straight upon the bed and the Phantom pointed to the head of the uncared-for body, unwatched, unwept, alone. The cover was so carelessly thrown over it that the slightest movement of Scrooge's finger could easily disclose the face. He half longed to do it but was powerless to move.

Oh cold, cold, rigid, dreadful Death!

This man lay in an empty house with not a man, woman or child to say that he had been kind to them. Only a cat was there, scratching at the door, and some rats who gnawed at the hearth stone.

"Spirit," begged Scrooge. "This is a fearful place. Let us go! If there is anyone who feels emotion at this man's death, please show him to me."

Then the Phantom spread its dark robe like a wing to reveal an anxious young mother, pacing the floor. At last her husband arrived and as soon as she had set his dinner before him, she could ask what news – was it good or bad?

"He is past relenting," explained her husband. "He is dead. I thought he made excuses to avoid me but he was truly ill. Still, now at least our debt may be transferred to a kinder creditor. We shall sleep tonight with light hearts."

"Oh, let me see some tenderness connected with a death," cried Scrooge.

So now the Ghost took Scrooge through several familiar streets to Bob Cratchit's house. Mrs Cratchit and the girls sat wearily sewing and sighing, while the little Cratchits, once so noisy, sat still as statues.

In came Bob, trying his best to be cheerful as the children rushed to help him to his tea. But then, as he talked of visiting Tiny Tim's grave, of how green a place it was and how he had promised Tiny Tim he would walk there every Sunday, Bob broke down and sobbed, "My little, little child, my little child!"

Once he had recovered the family drew about the fire and talked of how Bob had met Mr Scrooge's nephew who had

said many kind, sympathetic things.

"I am sure if you went and spoke with him, Mrs Cratchit," said Bob. "He would help find Peter some better employment."

Then the family kissed and hugged each other, knowing that whatever future separations there might be, the memory of poor Tiny Tim, of his sweet nature and patience, would remain a source of comfort and togetherness.

"We shall never forget poor Tiny Tim – or this first parting."

"Never, father!" cried they all.

"Spectre," said Scrooge, "I know not how I know but I feel our parting moment is at hand. Tell me what man that was whom we saw lying dead."

At this, the Ghost of Christmas Yet To Come hurried Scrooge away, through to the courtyard where Scrooge worked.

"I see the house," said Scrooge. "Why do you point away? Let me behold what I shall be, in days to come."

The Spirit stopped but his finger still pointed somewhere else, away from the familiar buildings. Scrooge peeped in the office window but the furniture was not the same and the figure in the chair was not himself. Still the Phantom pointed as before so Scrooge followed until they reached an iron gate and a churchyard beyond.

Here then lay the wretched man whose name he sought – in this most worthy place, walled in by houses, overgrown by grass and weeds made fat with too much burying.

The Spirit stood among the graves and pointed down to one.

"Before I draw near to that stone to which you point," said Scrooge, "answer me one question. Are these the shadows of the things that Will be, or shadows of things that May be, only?"

Still the Ghost pointed to the grave by which it stood.

"Men's courses will foreshadow certain ends. But if the courses be departed from, the ends will change. Say it is thus with what you show me," begged Scrooge again but the Spirit answered not. Scrooge crept towards the stone, trembling as he went. Following the finger of the Ghost, he looked down and there read his own name: EBENEZER SCROOGE.

"Am I that man who lay upon the bed?" cried Scrooge.

The finger pointed from the grave to Scrooge, and back again.

"No, Spirit!" cried Scrooge, clutching at his robe. "No! Hear me! I am not the man I was. Why show me this, if I am past hope? Assure me that I may yet change these shadows you have shown me, by an altered life! I will honour Christmas in my heart. I will live in the Past, the Present and the Future. Oh, tell me I may sponge away the writing on this stone."

In his agony, Scrooge caught the spectral hand and held on tightly but the Spirit was departing now and he was stronger than Scrooge could ever hope to hold. As Scrooge fell upon his knees, the Phantom's hood and dress shrunk, collapsed and dwindled into a bedpost.

Chapter Five

The End of It

Yes! The bedpost was his own, the bed his own, the room his own. Best and happiest of all, the Time was his own, to make amends in.

"The curtains are not torn down!" cried Scrooge, his face wet with tears; he was laughing and crying in the same breath. "Oh, Jacob Marley. Time be praised for this! I am light as a feather, happy as an angel, merry as a schoolboy." He frisked around the fireplace. "I don't know what day of the month it is," said Scrooge. "I don't how long I have been among the spirits. I'm quite a baby."

Hearing a lusty peal of bells, Scrooge flung the window open to glorious sunlight.

"What's today?" called Scrooge.

"Today," replied a boy below. "Why, it's CHRISTMAS DAY!"

"Christmas! I haven't missed it. The Spirits have done it all in one night," cried Scrooge. "My fine fellow, do you know the poulterers in the next street?"

"I should hope I did," replied the boy.

"An intelligent boy," said Scrooge. "Have they sold the prize turkey yet?"

"No. It's hanging there now."

"Go and buy it," said Scrooge. "I'll give you a shilling. Come back in less than five minutes and I'll make it half a crown."

The boy was off like a shot.

"I'll send it to Bob Cratchit's," laughed Scrooge. "It's twice the size of Tiny Tim. Hallo! Whoop! Hurrah!"

Then all was bustle. The enormous turkey was despatched to Bob Cratchit's and Scrooge set off with a chuckle along the streets. Soon he met the two gentlemen who had called at the counting house the previous day.

"Lord bless us!" they cried as Scrooge promised a huge donation. Then on he went, calling "Merry Christmas" to everyone, and "A Happy New Year to all the world", whooping and cheering until he reached his nephew's house.

"I have come to dinner!" Scrooge announced. "Will you let me in?"

"Why, bless my soul," cried Fred, but oh, what a wonderful party there was then! Wonderful games, wonderful happiness.

Scrooge was early at his office the next morning. The clock struck nine. No Bob. At last he arrived, some eighteen minutes late.

"What do you mean by arriving at this time of day?" growled Scrooge. "Step this way if you please."

"I am very sorry," pleaded Bob. "It's only once a year, sir. I was making rather merry yesterday."

"I am not going to stand this sort of thing any longer," said Scrooge. "In fact – I am going to raise your salary and care for your family. A Merry Christmas, Bob."

Scrooge was better than his word. He did it all, and more. And, with all this help, Tiny Tim did not die. Many remarked upon the change and from that time on, it was always said of Scrooge that he was a man who knew how to keep Christmas well.

And so, as Tiny Tim observed, "God bless us, every one!"